Nature's Cycles
Seasons

Los ciclos de la naturaleza
Las estaciones

Dana Meachen Rau

 **Marshall Cavendish**
Benchmark
New York

The year has four seasons: spring, summer, fall, and winter. You do different things in each season. Nature changes in each season, too.

El año tiene cuatro estaciones: primavera, verano, otoño e invierno. En cada estación, haces cosas diferentes. En cada estación, la naturaleza también cambia.

In spring, the air is warm. You can put away your hats and mittens. But you might need an umbrella!

En primavera, el aire es cálido. Puedes guardar tus gorros y tus guantes. ¡Pero tal vez necesites un paraguas!

Rainwater soaks into the ground. Seeds *sprout*. The new plants begin to grow up toward the sun.

———————❖———————

El agua de lluvia penetra en la tierra. Las semillas *germinan*. Las plantas nuevas empiezan a crecer hacia el sol.

Some animals wake up. They have slept all winter. Others animals return home. They have been in places where it was warm. Animals start looking for food. Birds begin to build nests.

Algunos animales se despiertan. Han dormido todo el invierno. Otros animales vuelven a su hogar. Han estado en lugares cálidos. Los animales empiezan a buscar alimento. Las aves empiezan a construir nidos.

Some animals have babies in spring.
Deer have fawns.

En primavera, algunos animales tienen crías.
Los ciervos tienen cervatillos.

Wolves have cubs. Mothers feed their babies to help them grow.

Los lobos tienen lobeznos. Las madres alimentan a sus crías para ayudarlas a crecer.

In summer, the air is hot. You have lots of time to play outside. The days are long. The nights are short.

En verano, el aire es caliente. Tienes mucho tiempo para jugar al aire libre. Los días son largos. Las noches son cortas.

The sun rises early and sets late. The sun is high in the sky in the middle of the day.

El sol sale temprano y se pone tarde. El sol está alto en el cielo a mediodía.

Summer storms can bring lightning and thunder. Dark clouds send rain.

Las tormentas de verano pueden traer rayos y truenos. Las nubes oscuras llevan lluvia.

Plants use the water to grow big and strong.
Flowers bloom in many colors.

———◆———

Las plantas usan el agua para crecer grandes y
fuertes. Las flores se abren de muchos colores.

Animals can find food easily in summer.
They drink water from ponds and creeks.

En verano, los animales encuentran alimento con facilidad. Beben agua de lagunas y arroyos.

Some cool off in puddles. You might cool off from the hot sun in a puddle, too!

———————❖———————

Algunos se refrescan en charcos. ¡Tú también podrías refrescarte del calor del sol en un charco!

In fall, the air is cool. Some plants die. Some leaves change color and fall to the ground. You might need to help rake them up.

En el otoño, el aire es fresco. Algunas plantas mueren. Algunas hojas cambian de color y caen al suelo. Tal vez necesites ayudar a rastrillarlas.

Animals get ready for winter by storing food. They also search for *shelter*. A chipmunk may find a *hollow* log.

❖

Los animales se preparan para el invierno almacenando alimento. También buscan *albergue*. Una ardilla listada puede encontrar un tronco *hueco*.

Frogs dig in mud under the water. A good shelter will keep them warm and safe when winter comes.

Las ranas excavan en el barro que está debajo del agua. Un buen albergue las mantendrá calientes y seguras cuando llegue el invierno.

Some birds *migrate* to warmer places in the fall. They fly in *flocks* together. They stop to rest and eat.

En otoño, algunos pájaros *migran* a lugares más cálidos. Vuelan juntos en *bandadas*. Se detienen para descansar y comer.

In winter, the air is cold. The days are short. The nights are long. The sun rises late and sets early. The sun is low in the sky. In some places, snow falls on the ground.

En invierno, el aire es frío. Los días son cortos. Las noches son largas. El sol sale tarde y se pone temprano. El sol está bajo en el cielo. En algunos lugares, cae nieve.

You can put on a warm coat to play outside.

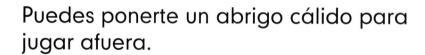

Puedes ponerte un abrigo cálido para
jugar afuera.

Some animals grow a warmer coat, too.
They search for food in the snow.

También, a algunos animales les crece un pelaje más abrigado. Buscan alimento en la nieve.

Other animals *hibernate*. They sleep all winter. Some animals just rest and eat the food they stored.

Many plants are *dormant* in winter. They are still alive, but they do not grow.

Otros animales *hibernan*. Duermen todo el invierno. Algunos animales simplemente descansan y comen el alimento que almacenaron.

En invierno, muchas plantas están *aletargadas*. Siguen vivas, pero no crecen.

Living things wait for spring to come. Nature will change again.

Los seres vivos esperan a que llegue la primavera. La naturaleza volverá a cambiar.

Challenge Words

dormant—Resting and not growing.

flocks—Groups of birds flying together.

hibernate—To sleep all winter.

hollow—Empty in the middle.

migrate—To travel to warmer places.

shelter—A safe place to live.

sprout—To begin to grow.

Palabras avanzadas

albergue—Un lugar seguro donde vivir.

aletargadas—Descansando y sin crecimiento.

bandadas—Grupos de pájaros que vuelan juntos.

germinar—Empezar a crecer.

hibernar—Dormir todo el invierno.

hueco—Vacío en el medio.

migrar—Viajar a lugares más cálidos.

Index

Page numbers in **boldface** are illustrations.

Índice

Las páginas indicadas con números en **negrita** tienen ilustraciones.

The author would like to thank Paula Meachen
for her scientific guidance and expertise in reviewing this book.
With thanks to Nanci Vargus, Ed.D.,
and Beth Walker Gambro, reading consultants.

Marshall Cavendish Benchmark
99 White Plains Road
Tarrytown, New York 10591
www.marshallcavendish.us

Library of Congress Cataloging-in-Publication Data

Rau, Dana Meachen, 1971–
[Seasons. Spanish & English]
Seasons = Las estaciones / Dana Meachen Rau.
p. cm. — (Bookworms. Nature's cycles = Los ciclos de la naturaleza)
Includes index.
Parallel text in English and Spanish; translated from the English.
ISBN 978-0-7614-4791-7 (bilingual ed.) — ISBN 978-0-7614-4098-7 (English ed.)
1. Seasons—Juvenile literature. I. Title. II. Title: Estaciones.
QB637.4.R3818 2010
508.2—dc22
2009019023

Editor: Christina Gardeski
Publisher: Michelle Bisson
Designer: Virginia Pope
Art Director: Anahid Hamparian

Spanish Translation and Text Composition by Victory Productions, Inc.
www.victoryprd.com

Photo Research by Anne Burns Images

Cover Photo by *Corbis*/Grafton Smith

The photographs in this book are used with permission and through the courtesy of:
Corbis: pp. 1, 16 Robert Llewellyn; p. 8 Tom Brakefield; p. 10 Rolf Bruderer; p. 23 Jorma Jamsen/zefa;
p. 28 Darrell Gulin. *Getty Images*: p. 2 Lori Adamski Peek; p. 13 Steve Satushek; p. 15 Juan Silva;
p. 24 Toshi Kawano. *Photo Edit*: p. 4 Bob Daemmrich. *Peter Arnold, Inc.*: p. 5 C. Huetter;
p. 7 PHONE Cordier Sylvain; p. 9 BIOS/J. Klein & M. Hubert; p. 11 R. Frank; p. 14 Patrick Frischknecht;
p. 18 Ed Reschke; p. 20 Johann Schumacher; p. 25 S. J. Krasemann; p. 27 WILDLIFE.
Photo Researchers: p. 12 Kent Wood; p. 19 Karl H. Switak.

Printed in Malaysia
1 3 5 6 4 2